An Introduction to Fox-Hunting

With Notes on Hunting Terms and Point-to-Point Races

By Major E. S. C. Hobson

Worcestershire Regiment

PANTIANOS
CLASSICS

Published by Pantianos Classics

ISBN-13: 978-1-78987-536-2

First published in 1911

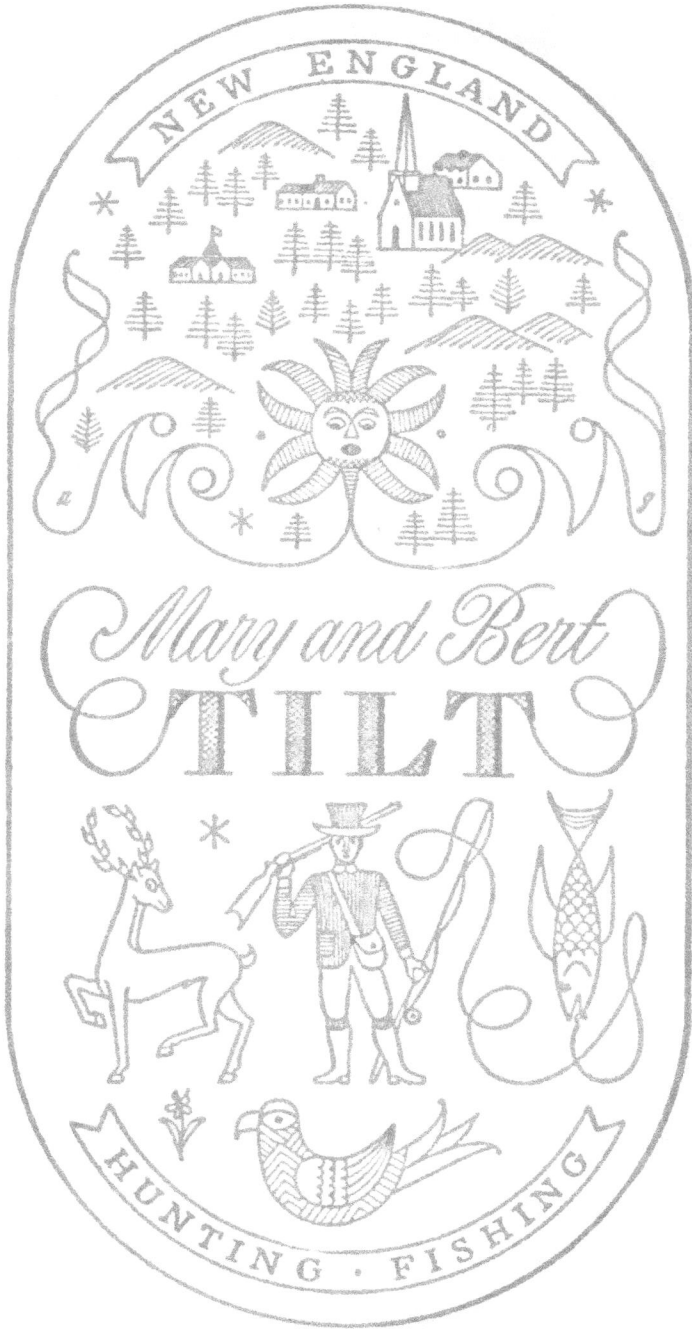

Advertisement from original edition, 1911

Contents

An Introduction to Fox-Hunting

Introduction

These notes on Fox-Hunting were originally intended to serve as a help to beginners in my own regiment. It has been suggested that they should be given a wider circulation, since so many young officers who desire to join in the sport lack previous experience in the Hunting Field, either from want of opportunity or lack of encouragement. These remarks, therefore, are not addressed to men with experience, but rather to the inexperienced people who come out hunting, and some of these are soldiers.

An idea of what is required can be gleaned from books, but experience alone can impress it on the mind. Horsemanship cannot be taught in books, nor can horse-mastery; both must be learned by practice. As a general rule officers are encouraged to take part in all Sports, because the experience and knowledge they acquire are invaluable to them as soldiers. The man who has been brought up in the atmosphere of country life and sport has a great advantage over his less fortunate brother officers, in managing and leading men; although if the qualities are there, experience may develop them.

I might begin by saying that running with beagles is an excellent schooling, but the opportunity of following the little hounds does not come to all of us.

Health and nerve are two such necessary qualities in fox-hunting, and both are so easily lost, that it is unnecessary to do more than to remark that the sportsman, whilst he should not shrink from acceptance of sporting risks, should never play tricks with his constitution. Loss of health means loss of nerve, and these gone, capacity for enjoyment is gone, so far as hunting is concerned.

August to November

The importance of conditioning hunters at this time of the year is, in many cases, overlooked altogether or insufficiently carried out. If horses are to be called upon to do a hard season's work, they must start with hard flesh on them, and the bigger they are at this time of the year the better. Two months of long slow exercise, walking and jogging for two to four hours a day, with an extra feed of oats per day, and gradually increased as work increases, will bring horses out fit to go all day in November. A few gallops will soon put their wind right. Let them drink as much water as they want, and always before food, if you do not adopt the plan of leaving a bucket of water in the box at all times. It takes longer to condition a horse that has been turned out in summer, than one that has been in a straw yard.

Horses require clipping at this time of the year. Most people clip them all over the first time, but the second time, some leave the saddle mark and the legs undipped. The saddle mark is useless if your saddle fits properly; it is intended to take the place, in a measure, of a numnah, while the hair on the legs is usually left as a protection from thorns. If horses are turned out in the summer, it is a pity to hog their mane, or have them docked, as the mane and tail are their principal means of warding off flies.

If your shoeing is well done, you should not lose many shoes in a season. If you lose a shoe out hunting, bring the horse home, keeping him as far as possible on soft ground. Always on arriving at the Meet look to see if all your horse's shoes are on.

Overhaul all your tackle, and see that everything is in good order for the coming season. Singeing will remove all ragged hairs left after clipping, and the horse should then be given a water brushing all over.

Look always to your bridle and girths before mounting; see that bit and bridoon are in their right places, that the curb chain lies evenly in its place and is not too tight or too slack, also that the throat lash is not too tight. When mounted, bring your right leg forward, lift the saddle flap, look to your girths, and if necessary gently draw them up before you start. Some horses "blow themselves out" when the groom is saddling them; in most cases the girths need drawing up a hole or two when your weight is in the saddle.

Never lend a horse to a nervous man who will allow him to refuse, or who has not good hands and an even temper, as he is likely to spoil the best mannered hunter.

You are not particularly wanted out cubbing, as the hunt servants have different work to do from that which they have to perform after October. Cub-hunting is not the occasion for you to school horses or lark over fences.

If you are asked by the Master to help to hold up a cub, stand well out in the field where you can be seen, and turn the cub back into covert.

Be careful not to get amongst hounds going to Cry, as at this time of the year horses are fresh and liable to kick.

Remember the ground you are on is the farmer's; should a farmer ask you not to go over a certain place, comply at once with his wishes, even if hounds are running; he is entitled to respect, and if treated in an off-hand manner may put up wire. Moreover, he may be the owner of the land. Use a gap if one exists, but never make one.

Be particularly careful to close gates behind you, lest stock stray and cause the farmer needless trouble.

Be tolerant with shooting men; they can help your sport, and you should respect theirs; shooting men own many of the coverts in every hunt, and their interests must be studied if their goodwill is to be engaged on behalf of fox-preservation.

Treat pedestrians with respect, they may be poor and unable to mount themselves, but perhaps know more of the sport in hand than you do, and may have a vested interest in the Hunt.

Bear in mind that all are welcome in the hunting field, and whether on foot or mounted all are on the same plane as sportsmen.

When you hear a hulloa, look towards the horizon, and bring your eye in, to view a fox that has broken covert. Never go into small coverts while hounds are drawing; but in large coverts it is advisable if the Master allows it, as by so doing you can see and hear what hounds are doing, and can get away on good terms with them if they go away.

You will always find someone who is willing to give you advice as to a short cut home, or to a meet. Unless you have an eye for a country, or a knowledge of the country you are in, you will perhaps save yourself time and trouble if you keep to the road.

If you get your horse in a bog, do not try to turn him round, but flog him out on the far side, otherwise you may strain him.

The ground is often as hard in the cubbing season as when there is frost; it jars horses' legs and feet to be galloped on hard ground, and may ruin them, while on frozen ground there is the additional danger of slipping.

Never argue with the Master if reprimanded; he is most likely right, but if he is wrong he will apologise on the first opportunity; if you are wrong you should apologise. Remember that the M.F.H. has much to try him and is supreme in the Hunting Field.

November to April

Always be punctual at the meet. Hounds may find an outlying fox, or go to some unusual covert to draw, and you then have to go and find them. Six miles an hour is a good pace to allow going to the meet.

Let your horse stale when you arrive; some horses stale more readily on straw or with a little straw shaken underneath them.

Never keep a horse standing about waiting for you.

When hounds pass you on the road, stop and turn your horse's head towards them.

While hounds are drawing a covert, go where the Master orders the Field; do not try to get a start unfairly, as it may spoil everyone's sport.

In a large covert, go inside and listen where hounds are, and what they are doing.

When watching a ride never take your eyes off it, as the fox will probably cross at the very moment you do so.

Never speak to the Whips outside a covert, they have their work to do, and you must not take their attention from it.

If you view a fox away, let him get through the next fence, or count twenty slowly before you holloa; do not move, or holloa too soon, or he will go back into covert. If you see hounds go away on a fox that you have not viewed, do not holloa, but shout "Tally ho Forard Away."

Keep your eye on the leading hounds, they are carrying the line.

Don't ride to every halloa you hear; use discretion and try and hear where the Huntsman and hounds are, and be guided by their movements.

Don't break down fences or locked gates; the latter can sometimes be taken off their hinges and closed again; never leave a gate hanging by the chain or on the ground.

A padlock can be opened with a stirrup iron if the gate cannot be lifted off its hinges; but this is an experiment to which you should rarely have recourse.

Never ride too near to hounds, nor directly in their wake, but ride wide of them to right or left, nor "in the pocket" of a hunt servant. And never jump a fence near a hound.

Always stop when hounds check, and remain still while they are casting, or while the Huntsman makes his cast, and watch what they are doing. It is advisable not to hulloa at this period if you get a view, as it gets hounds' heads up; it is better to hold up your hat.

The steam from hot horses foils the ground, so do not move about on ground where the Huntsman may want to cast.

When hounds check, try and discover the reason. Villages, men at plough or working in a field, heavily manured land, or a stray dog will all cause checks, and the latter will turn a fox from his point.

Cattle, sheep or colts crossing a fox's line will also cause a check by foiling the ground.

If you view a fox, never hulloa unless you are certain it is the one the hounds are hunting, as there may be several on foot, and you will get the hounds' heads up from the one they are hunting.

Sheep staring or circling, also cattle or colts staring, may probably denote the presence of a fox. Rooks will often circle over a beaten fox.

When after a hunt, the fox begins to twist and turn, look out for a view and a kill.

At a kill, or when digging a fox out, keep at a distance; horses dislike the smell of blood, and will kick hounds.

Always give way to the Huntsman and any of the hunt servants; they all have their work to do, and unless done properly you will get no sport. Treat them with every consideration, as their day's work is much longer than your day's pleasure.

Small tips to anyone who does you a service, like opening a gate for you, are well spent, and encourage the recipient to help your sport. Also spend freely within your means when it may promote hunting.

If on your way home, or at any other time during the day, you find stock or colts straying on the road, do not drive them, but turn them into the first enclosure you find, and tell somebody living near that you have done so.

Always be careful not to injure lambs; if it is necessary to carry them out of danger, pick them up by the two fore legs with one hand, holding them close up to the shoulders, and put them in a place of safety.

Never forget to close all open gates.

Do not pull at a horse's mouth; remember that if you pull at him he will pull at you.

In a run remember that wide places require more pace to get over them. If you see hounds jump in and out of water, you will want to put more pace on, as it is sure to be wide. Ride at all fences at a fair pace, but not fast at timber. Some people prefer to ride at timber at a slant, but there is no object in doing so.

With a tired horse avoid timber, and only jump when absolutely necessary. A tired horse rushes his fences and gives bad falls, and will not be in a hurry to get up if he falls on you.

Never take unnecessary jumps; it looks bad, you do damage, tire your horse, and you may bring a willing horse down. Never refuse the help of a gate if it does not take you out of your way; it is not at all necessary to be always jumping in order to get to hounds.

In fallow fields keep to the headland that has been left on purpose for you, and ride down furrows and ridges rather than across them. Furrows with water standing in them have generally the soundest bottoms.

When hounds check, turn your horse's head to the wind. Get off your horse when they kill and whenever else you can, to ease his back. It eases his back and yourself to get off and walk down steep hills going home. If your horse is getting a sore back put your woollen gloves under the saddle, one on each side of the place where it is chafed. This will prevent it getting worse.

Do not turn homewards while hounds are running, but do not keep one horse out too long. If he is away from his stable for seven or eight hours he has done a good day's work, and will come out again all the sooner.

A bucket of gruel and a mouthful of hay will always help your horse on his journey home; make sure that a clean pail is used. This should be given under your own supervision, and before thinking of your own comfort. If oatmeal is used, it should be mixed in cold water before the tepid water is added. Failing the gruel, give him a drink at a stream. Keep him moving all the way home. Horses that are tired come home better in company than alone. If you call at a house on the way home for refreshment, remember your horse and also the man who looked after him. A bottle of beer or half a bottle of whisky in the horse's gruel may be added if he is very tired.

There is no harm in letting a horse graze at odd moments out hunting; it will probably do him good.

If a stray hound should follow you home, shut him up and return him next day, after feeding and bedding him clown. It is very bad for a hound to be left out all night.

There is always something to be learned out hunting, so watch the hunt servants, watch the good men, watch the hounds, and try and learn something of their art of Hunting. All you can learn is to your advantage.

Also learn the various meanings of the notes on the horn, so that when the huntsman touches his horn it will convey some information to you, as it is intended to do.

Stable Management

Forage, Grooms, Tackle, etc.

In infantry regiments, as a rule, soldier grooms are false economy. It is not their job, or they would not be soldiers, and it is impossible to convince them of their ignorance. If you can afford it, buy sound horses and made horses that know their business. They will help to teach you. It is no good having both man and horse ignorant of their work. Made horses require no schooling and dislike being larked over fences, and should you lame your horse when playing the fool you have no one to thank but yourself.

Young horses are of no use to beginners, nor can you get the same amount of work out of them as out of aged horses. Horses that have been coaching in the summer are sure to be in hard condition, and they have had no weight on their backs. In buying you must be guided by your purse, but get them up to your weight. If they are not up to your weight you are very apt to break them down.

In buying cheap horses, do not get a screw with a back tendon or suspensory ligament gone. Curbs on old horses, especially if they have been fired, are not so likely to give trouble as on young horses. You want to start with four legs, so buy a horse that is sound; but do not mind blemishes if the price suits. Lots of fun can be had on a horse gone in his wind if he suits in other respects; but of course screws will not fetch much more when you sell them than the price given for them. Good sound horses will always fetch their price, which will probably be beyond your means.

When buying, carry in your mind the stamp of horse you require, and get one suited to the country you are going to hunt in.

Keep a saddle that fits him, for each horse. Get good tackle, and it will last longest.

Ride each horse in the bit that suits him best.

Summering hunters is a matter upon which authorities are not always agreed. They can be (1) either kept up and hacked or driven; (2) put in a straw yard; or (3) turned out to grass. This last, however, is not to be recommended for horses gone in the wind; horses turned out to grass also lose all their condition, whereas they do not under either of the first two methods of summering. If the second or third method be adopted, the horse should have a feed of corn every day, and in the straw yard and stable a bundle of vetches also.

During the season in full work a big horse will do with three or four feeds a day, and should always have what water he will drink, and on hunting days one or two feeds before starting. Horses should always be watered *before* being fed.

It will pay you to buy the best forage; buy either from farmers or contractors. The latter will deliver you smaller quantities if your stud is small; but give the farmer your custom if you can.

I am a firm believer in giving chaff with every feed of oats; it makes a horse chew his oats, and puts a barrell on him.

Plenty of fresh air and grooming will put bloom on his coat; avoid draughts and stuffy stables.

Linseed gruel is excellent on returning from hunting, and you should give the seeds afterwards in a hot mash.

If it is necessary to physic a horse, soft food in the shape of a mash should be given before and after it; not hard food.

Never take the saddle off the moment the horse come in, as this practice is conducive to sore backs; slacken the girths and let it remain on for half-an-hour.

Numnahs are not necessary if the saddle is well stuffed and is dried and brushed regularly and thoroughly, but if you use a numnah, the best one is of plain leather, with holes punched in it on both sides at the top from front to rear, kept clean and soft with oil.

Flannel bandages put on after hunting keep the legs warm; while a hot wet flannel bandage with the water squeezed out, with a dry one on top of it, will bring down inflammation.

If a horse has cold ears, they should be pulled until warmth returns.

Hand rubbing is the best thing for legs. The legs should be well searched for thorns after hunting. Dirt should be brushed off when dry. Do not use water on your horse's legs, unless you are certain your groom will dry them afterwards.

Cracked heels and thrush are due to neglect in the stable.

Lameness in a horse can be detected by watching his ears. If he is lame in front, he drops his head when the sound leg comes to the ground, so as to throw the weight on it. The action is *vice versa* if he is lame behind. If he is lame in the foot, it can be ascertained by tapping the hoof with a hammer. If lame in the shoulder, he flinches when the leg is pulled out straight to the front.

Always put clothing on, though not too much, when sending a horse by train. Hoods, except for long railway journeys, are unnecessary.

Have a bag in which to leave your own coat and horse rug at the end of the journey, if you are boxing to a meet.

If your clothing gets lost, and you have to box your horse home without any, put him in the centre stall of the box, between two other horses to keep him warm. I do not advise borrowing rugs from a public yard.

Hunters do better in a box than in a stall, where they can lie down and rest themselves, and after a day's hunting, can give themselves all the exercise they require.

Straw put down thick and well banked up against the sides of the box is the best bedding for all horses.

Always let your horse cool down before bringing him into the stable, or he will break out.

When returning home, walk the last mile or so, in order that your horse may come in cool. If a horse comes in hot, have him walked about till he is cool.

With ordinary luck a horse should do three days' hunting a fortnight.

Twisting the stirrup leathers towards the horse's tail will make the irons hang in an easy position to find with your foot.

When leading a horse, always turn your face from him, and walk on; never turn round and face him.

String or woollen gloves should be carried under the saddle flap to put on in wet or cold weather. String gloves are the best for wet weather, and are cool.

Always ride in the most comfortable position to yourself, but the shorter your leathers are the more your weight will be thrown back.

Should you gall your knees, riding straps over them will protect the skin from worse rubbing.

If a horse is down, and not inclined to get up, stretch his fore legs out straight in front of him, and then try and get him to rise.

In the event of fire breaking out in a stable, horses should be led quietly out as if nothing extraordinary had happened; if time allows, put a saddle on them to make it seem more usual to them.

Shoeing. — The horse should be shod whenever it is necessary, but the shoes should be removed every month. Great care should be taken with the shoeing. The wall of the hoof gets thinner from the toe to the heel, and is continued from there to the centre of the foot by bars, and between the bars comes the frog. Not more of the wall should be cut away than is necessary, and the same applies to the sole of the foot. The bars also should not be cut too much, as they and the wall bear all the weight. No sound part of the frog should be cut away.

Hay. — There are always a few weeds, even in good hay. Always buy old hay; new hay is moist, and can be recognised by its feel, smell, and appearance; it looks fresh and green.

Straw. — Wheat straw is the best, and should be long, dry and clean.

Oats. — White oats are better than black. Always buy old oats, which should be hard, clean and thin of husk. New oats smell fresh, and taste sweet and juicy; they are softer than old oats. The kernel of old oats is smooth, and that of new oats, furry. Crushed oats are easier to digest than whole grain.

Bran. — This should be clean, dry and fresh.

Some General Hints

The question of subscriptions to hunts for soldiers who hunt where they are quartered should not be difficult, as a regimental subscription, including each individual's contribution, is always gladly accepted. Away from the headquarters of a regiment, £5 per horse per day a week, and £2 or £3 to poultry funds may be taken as a sufficient subscription per season in small hunts, but a regular tariff is now drawn up in most of the larger hunts, or fashionable packs, as they are called; but then you need not be fashionable until you can afford it. Before going to a new country, it is best to write to the Secretary and ask him for all information on this subject.

It may perhaps not be out of place here to mention the Christmas tips to the hunt servants of the pack with which you have been hunting. £2 or £3 to the Huntsman and £1 each to the Whips would be ample, and should certainly not be less than half these amounts.

The trophies of the chase may be looked upon as the perquisites of the hunt servants, and £1 for the brush or mask and 10*s*. for the pad will meet the case; but again, I would suggest, certainly not less than half those amounts. If your hunt goes in for capping, always have your money ready for the collector. Readiness helps him in his task, which is a very thankless one. In Ireland they always cap.

Make a rule of hunting where and when you can, and if you can afford it, six days a week up to Christmas, and as many days after as possible.

Never stay at home on a hunting day on account of rain, or you may miss a good day's sport. Do not pick your meets, as good sport may be had from the most unlikely places. If you hunt regularly with one pack you are sure of getting all their sport.

Spurs certainly set a boot off, but, to most people, are just as useful without rowels. Blunt rowels, or none, moreover, may save you getting into trouble with your horse. The only correct uniform for fox-hunting is a pink coat, with a plain button (unless you are entitled to wear a hunt button) when the season commences, and the evening dress on and after the opening meet of your hunt.

A tall hat is the correct headdress, and is a great protection against blows from branches and in the event of a fall. Besides, it is only due to the Master that you should pay him the compliment of being properly dressed. To take your hat off to him on your arrival at the meet is a courtesy due to the M.F.H.

It is extraordinary how often men carry their crops clumsily. Always have a thong on your crop, and let the thong hang down straight or coiled, grasping it and the crop about half-way up the crop, with the handle downwards. Do not carry a cutting whip.

Have your reins sewn on to the bits; never have buckles on your bridle.

Never ride across polo grounds, lawns, cricket grounds, golf course, or grass borders.

Never ride over seeds, or roots; with seeds, water stands in the hoof-mark and rots them; with roots, you cut them, and after frost they rot. Beans suffer most from being ridden over.

Always wait your turn at a gap or in a gateway; but if hounds are running, have a go at the fence and save time.

Always push or swing open a gate with your crop, held in the proper hand, i.e., the hand that is nearest the hinges. One ought never to lose time at a gate, or keep others waiting. Never let a gate slam on the person behind; you would not like it done to you. Do not push in a crowded gateway.

If your horse kicks, keep him clear of crowds, tie a red tape on his tail, and if other people crowd up on you, put you hand behind your back as a warning to them.

Do not let your horse tread on the heels of a horse in front of him, or touch another horse's quarters with his head.

Horses should not be suffered to paw in mud and water as it splashes other people.

Never let a horse lie down with a saddle on, or he will roll and break the tree; if he does get down, flog him up.

If your horse takes to bolting or rearing, either sell or shoot him; the latter for choice.

A pink coat always commands respect, but some wearers of pink are ignorant about hunting, and are not necessarily good pilots.

If you are following a pilot always give him plenty of room at his fences in case he falls, so that you may not then jump on him.

Should you notice a hole, broken glass, or wire, that may cause injury, always give warning of its presence by shouting "Ware wire!" or "Ware hole!"

Take the time when you find a fox, and when the hunt is over, you can then compare runs.

If you lose hounds during the day, remember that horses locate sound easier than men; your horse may locate them for you, if you watch his ears.

It is a bad practice to go coffee-housing, as you may lose hounds, and never see them again that day.

Look for pad marks of hounds, to see if they have gone down a road in front of you.

It is not necessary to pull up when anyone falls, unless you see he wants help. It is quite sufficient to ask if he is all right, and if told he is not hurt, catch his horse, and hang the reins over the nearest gate-post, or, if time allows, take it back to him. Another man will always do the same for you. If a man is down and in danger of being kicked, put your own saddle over his head.

Colts, cattle or sheep when frightened will stampede and break through a fence, possibly hurting themselves, and always giving the trouble of collecting them; they may also cost the owner the expense of getting them out of the local pound; always try to prevent colts or stock from breaking fences.

Don't offer assistance to the Huntsman, as there are servants paid to do so, and you will not be thanked for interfering. Do not press on hounds when following them on the road. If they pass you, let the thong of your crop hang down towards them, and they will then avoid your horse.

When driving along a road, if you meet hounds, always pull up to let them pass you.

Never take a short cut through a covert that is to be drawn during the day, for fear of disturbing it. Do not start to ride home near a covert that hounds are drawing, for fear of heading the fox. Do not throw sandwich paper about; it may frighten a horse, and it annoys land owners.

Never stop at public houses, and never allow your groom to do so.

To dry a damp lucifer match, rub it in your hair for a few seconds, when it will strike.

Take your sport wherever you can get it; with a drag hunt, if you can get no other; it is not true sport, but it sharpens you up.

Be civil to countrymen, even if they give you bad information, and always reply to their enquiries as to "did you kill," etc.

If you have a second horse out, make your second horseman keep with the hunt second horses, and close all open gates; he should never jump.

It is unnecessary to talk of your doings; if you held a prominent place in a hunt, you have the satisfaction of knowing that you enjoyed yourself; you have certainly been seen and probably envied.

It is customary where, overtaking a Hunt on the road, in a motor car, not to sound your horn unless it is necessary to give notice of your presence, but to slow down to their pace, and wait till the road is clear for you to proceed.

Some Hunting Terms

The point of a run is the distance between the two points in the run that are farthest apart. "Scoring to the cry" is when hounds are all throwing their tongues. In "full cry" they are heads up and sterns down, and have not time nor breath to throw their tongues much. "Flashing" is when hounds go beyond the line of a fox, generally when they are pressed on by horsemen. "Driving" is when they dash on to take up the scent farther on and save close hunting, a great attribute in a hound. "Babbling" is throwing tongue unnecessarily. A hound is said to "skirt" when he keeps away from the body of the pack. "Riot" is the pursuit of hares, rabbits, or deer, rather than fox. The "drag" of a fox is where he moved about overnight. The "billet" of a fox is his dung. The "kennel" is where he slept at night. "Running mute" is when a hound is hunting, but will not open and throw his tongue. An "outlying fox" is one that for the time has taken up his quarters away from a covert. A fox's head is called a "mask," his tail a "brush," and his foot a "pad." The hound's tail is called his "stern." "Breaking up" a fox is the "tear and eat him" part of the obsequies. Hounds will not break up a mangy fox. "Casting" hounds is helping them to hit off again the line they have lost. An "oxer" is a single wooden rail some four feet from a fence to keep the cattle from the fence; there may also be a ditch as well. When a Huntsman catches hold of some of his hounds in cover and gets the fox between them and the body of the pack, he is said to "throw them in at the head," a device used chiefly in cubbing. "Feathering" is when hounds are puzzling out a line, but are not sufficiently certain to open and speak to it.

Point-To-Point Races

In most hunts at the end of the season, Point-to-Point races are held over a line of country; and the man who owns a horse of any merit in his own country likes to enter and ride him. In grass countries and in the Shires, a horse with more quality and scope is required than in close and more cultivated countries. In most Point-to-Point races, the course is quite clearly marked with turning flags, and in many cases competitors are allowed to walk over the course, so that in any case no one should lose his way, hence it practically resolves itself into a steeplechase. Should the grass country hunter, who may be three parts bred and next door to a race horse, meet under these conditions the honest but slow hunter, from more provincial hunts, the latter will be no match for the former as long as he does not fall. It is therefore as well, before entering your horse, to know something of the company he will have to meet.

It takes a good horse to win a Point-to-Point at the present time; he must be able to gallop, stay the course, jump quickly without losing ground at his fences— all qualities of the racehorse. He must in addition have the handy qualities of the hunter. There are good horsemen and good men to hounds in every hunt, and these men, suitably mounted, would go well in any country. There are also in every hunt men whose ambition it is to win their local Point-to-Point, and to run their horses at neighbouring hunt races also. These men realise that the horse they select for Point-to-Point work must combine all the necessary qualities, and although they may not see more or as much fun with him out hunting as they do with their other horses, at Point-to-Point work he is in a different class from the rest of the stud.

In riding Point-to-Point races, it is quite as important as in race-riding that the man should be as fit as his horse. Some men cannot keep their top hats on, and wear racing caps instead, but this should not be necessary; it is not necessary out hunting, and these races are generally run in hunting costume. I am inclined to think that of two horses, one slightly ahead of the other when coming to their fence stride for stride, the one in the rear is more likely to fall through taking off just when the leading horse does. This liability does not exist when there is a length or more between them. A horse loses ground when he changes his feet. Undoubtedly the place to make ground is down hill, and the horse that is sent along down hill will not lose through it. There are many opportunities of noticing how other horses are going. A whip is of no use except in a close finish, and then only in the last few strides, and a horse should be hit behind the girths just as his hind legs come to the ground, so that he may make a more determined push off with them in his next stride.

If it is allowed, always walk over a course that you are going to ride over, and note where the going is good or bad, and where you should have each fence.

Where walking over the course is not allowed, it is very necessary to make up your mind quickly, on entering a field, at which place you mean to jump out of it; and with your mind made up on this head, let nothing turn you from it.

Always he well up with your horses, and avoid getting behind or near a known refuser; also, let a loose horse have plenty of room.

Do not sacrifice any of your season's sport for the sake of one ride in a Point-to-Point.

At the start have your horse collected, well balanced, and with his head facing the right way, so that you can get off at once. Keep your eyes on the starter.

Do not race with every horse that comes alongside you during a race, but towards the end when the pace quickens, you must go along with them, and not take a pull at your fences. Always have your horse collected, and have a feel of his mouth, never let him sprawl.

Do not whip or spur a horse just as he is going to take off at a fence, but squeeze him with your knees. Keep both hands down, and on the reins in front of you. Never raise your right hand going over a fence. It is a matter of choice, whether you run your horse in racing plates or in his own light hunting shoes.

Advertisement from the original edition, 1911

40

www.ingramcontent.com/pod-product-compliance
Lightning Source LLC
Chambersburg PA
CBHW021921040426
42448CB00007B/859